P9-BZL-051

BOOK NEWS

JULIAN MESSNER
Division of Simon & Schuster, Inc.
1 WEST 39th STREET   NEW YORK 10018
TELEPHONE 212-245-6400

Selected Reviews on

THE YELLOW RIVER
by Margaret Rau; illustrated by Haris Petie

"This is a well written book for younger students
and includes maps, index, and word pronunciation.
It covers much Chinese history and culture as well
as the geography of the Yellow River. Binding,
paper, printing and illustrations are superior."
                         Association of Children's
                         Librarians of No. California

"This is an interesting story of the Yellow River
that is often referred to as 'China's Sorrow' because of its dangerous floods. This river is also
the mainstay of millions of Chinese. The book de-
scribes the river as it follows its course through
the country where it helps the farmer as well as
the factory owner. The author was born in China
and has an accurate understanding of her people
and the country. Valuable as a social studies re-
ference."   Wisconsin "Book Gleanings"

"...offers a delightful way to learn geography as
well as history linked to current events. One section tells how to pronounce the Chinese place
names involved....The book carries a special line
of acknowledgment to Mrs. Man-Hing Yue Mok, head
of the Oriental Library at UCLA."
                         "Books for the Family"
                         by Ruth C. Ikerman
                         Los Angeles Times

THE YELLOW RIVER

Books by Margaret Rau

The Yellow River

The Band of the Red Hand

Dawn from the West:
    The Story of Genevieve Caulfield

The Penguin Book

THE
YELLOW
RIVER

by MARGARET RAU

Illustrated by Haris Petie

JULIAN MESSNER NEW YORK

Published simultaneously in the United States and Canada by
Julian Messner, a division of Simon & Schuster, Inc.,
1 West 39 Street, New York, N.Y. 10018. All rights reserved.

Copyright, ©, 1969 by Margaret Rau

Printed in the United States of America
SBN 671-32125-0 TRADE
671-32125-9 MCE
Library of Congress Catalog Card No. 69-12117
Designed by Marjorie Zaum K.

.915.11
j R239y

For
Loretta and Lucia Hwong

99699

ACKNOWLEDGMENT

I wish to thank Mrs. Man-Hing Yue Mok, Head of the Oriental Library at the University of California, Los Angeles, for her interest in THE YELLOW RIVER.

Contents

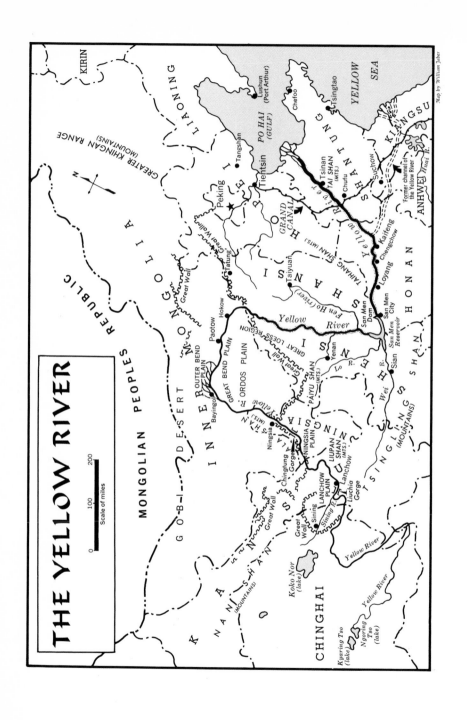

THE YELLOW RIVER

Scale of miles
0   100   200

KIRIN

LIAONING

GREATER KHINGAN RANGE (MOUNTAINS)

MONGOLIAN PEOPLES REPUBLIC

G O B I D E S E R T

INNER MONGOLIA

PO HAI (GULF)

Lushun (Port Arthur)
Chefoo
Tsingtao

YELLOW SEA

KIANGSU

Tangshan
Tientsin
Peking

Great Wall

Tatung
Hokow
Paotow

OUTER BEND PLAIN
Bayingol
GREAT BEND PLAIN
ORDOS PLAIN

Great Wall

GREAT LOESS REGION

Yellow River

Taiyuan

Fen Ho (river)

SHANSI

SHANTUNG
Tsinan
TAI SHAN (MTS.)
Chufu
Suchow

GRAND CANAL

TAIHANG SHAN (MTS.)
Kaifeng
Chengchow
Loyang

HONAN

Former channel of the Yellow River

ANHWEI Huai R.

San Men Dam
San Men City
San Men Reservoir

Yellow River

HOPEH

PAIYU SHAN (MTS.)

Yenan

Lo R.

HELAN SHAN (MTS.)

Ningsia
NINGSIA PLAIN
(LIUPAN SHAN (MTS.)

Chingtung Gorge

LANCHOW PLAIN
Lanchow

Sining
Sining R.

Liuchia Gorge

Wei R.
Sian

SHENSI

TSINGLING SHAN (MOUNTAINS)

KANSU

Great Wall

NAN SHAN (MOUNTAINS)

Koko Nor (lake)

CHINGHAI

Kyaring Tso (lake)
Ngoring Tso (lake)

Yellow River

Yellow River

Map by William Jaber

The Land of the Yak

The Yellow River, or Hwang Ho, as it is called in Chinese, is one of three great rivers, all of which flow across China from the highlands in the west to the Pacific Ocean in the east. The other two rivers are the Yangtze, which crosses central China, and the Si-Kiang, which crosses southern China.

The Yellow River crosses northern China. Like its sister river the Yangtze, it rises in the rugged province of Chinghai. Chinghai separates northern and central China from Tibet, which lies to the west. Sometimes Chinghai has belonged to Tibet and sometimes to China. Today it is part of Communist China, which also rules Tibet.

The birthplace of the Yellow River lies almost fifteen

9

thousand feet above sea level in the heart of the towering Kunlun Mountains. Here in a remote valley lies a chain of lakes and marshlands linked by meandering streams. As the streams flow eastward, they gradually unite to form a single shallow river several yards wide and a foot or so deep. This is the beginning of the Yellow River. Its waters here are crystal clear and as green as pale jade.

Beyond the valley, steppelands stretch away for miles on all sides. "Steppe" is a Russian word for a broad treeless plain. These steppes are called the Great Grass Desert. The Grass Desert has too little water for human beings to live there. But it is the home of many wild animals and birds.

In the winter, the steppes are especially desolate. Then the streams and marshes that feed the Yellow River are frozen solid. Blizzards sweep down from the high mountains, covering the Grass Desert with snow. The temperature drops below zero.

Spring brings a kinder look to the vast lonely lands. The geese, golden-eyed ducks, and sheldrakes return to their nesting grounds in the Yellow River swamps. Thousands of tawny marmots and black mouse hares with orange-tipped ears pop out of their burrows which honeycomb the hill slopes. They sit in their doorways in the sun, their heads cocked for danger. At the first sign of it, they will rush, trilling and squeaking, back into their holes. They

have many enemies—hawks and eagles, weasels and foxes. Even the yellowish-brown steppe bears, who waken from their winter hibernation, prey on the little creatures.

The wolves and the leopards of the Great Grass Desert stalk larger game—deer and antelope. But they seldom can bring down the Tibetan wild ass that roams these steppes.

The Tibetan wild ass does not resemble the homely tame ass we know, though its ears are as long. Its coat is yellowish brown, fading to white over the belly. Its legs are almost white, and a narrow dark stripe runs down its back. It is so swift and graceful that the old Tibetans believe it is the steed of the gods. Because of this, they regard killing a wild ass as a very serious matter.

Rainfall on the Chinghai steppes comes in summertime and often falls in torrents. Then the Yellow River becomes swollen with angry water which carries along a heavy load of silt stripped from the Tibetan highlands. Turned to a muddy yellow by this silt, the river rushes eastward through wild and lonely gorges.

After flowing in this direction for four hundred miles, it loops back to take a westerly direction. The bend that it makes waters the home of the Ngolo tribe. In the past the Ngolo tribesmen were among the most feared in all Asia. They were a tough, fierce bandit people who raided the caravans that came their way.

The caravan pack animals were yaks, and to a Tibetan the yak is the most important animal in the world. He looks quite silly with his long thick hair and very short legs. Tufts of hair below his knees give him the appearance of a gigantic poodle. Even his tail has a tuft of hair at the end, and he often uses it as a flyswatter. Despite his sharp fierce-looking horns, he has a gentle face.

The yak supplies the Tibetan herdsmen with almost everything they need. It provides butter, yogurt, buttermilk and cheese, and on very rare occasions some yak steaks. It provides hair cloth for tents, clothes, and bedding. It has also served as a pack animal for centuries.

As a pack animal, however, the yak is not very efficient. It is slow, somewhat stupid, and given to throwing its load whenever it chooses. A caravan of yaks could be easily stampeded by the Ngolo tribesmen. The booty they acquired was valuable, especially if the caravans belonged to merchants. Tea, silks, silver, gold, grains, and, of course, the yaks themselves would fall into the hands of the bandits.

In recent years highways have been built enabling trucks instead of caravans to transport goods. And the Ngolo tribe has settled down to a peaceful life of yak herding.

For another hundred miles the Yellow River continues its journey through steep winding gorges. Then it turns northward and comes out into open steppelands again. It has left the Great Grass Desert behind. The high plateau through which it is flowing now is inhabited by the Panaka nomads, who live west of the river.

Nomads are shepherd people who do not have fixed homes but wander from place to place pitching their tents wherever they can find pasturage for their herds.

The tents of the Panaka nomads are made of woven yak hair and dot the land like colonies of great black spiders. Their herds of yak number in the thousands, and they have many thousands of goats and sheep as well.

The Panaka men are tall and straight. They wear cloaks of sheepskin with the wool turned inward for warmth. These cloaks are called *shubas*. Their felt hats have high conical crowns which they wear tilted to one side. Their straight black hair hangs loose to their shoulders. Their

boots are made of yak cloth with raw yakhide soles.

The women wear shubas and boots, too. They plait their hair in one hundred and eight slender braids, tying all the ends together with gay ribbons. They wear wide strips of gray or black cloth hanging down their back and fastened round their neck with a cord. These strips are ornamented with huge silver knobs that look like bowls turned upside down. Often the knobs are eight inches across and four inches high and are quite heavy. But no self-respecting older Panaka woman would be seen without this decoration, even when she is working. The younger women, however, are beginning to dress more comfortably and to wear their hair in simple styles.

If you were to drop in on the Panaka nomads at mealtime, you would find them eating tea soup and tsamba. The tea soup is made by brewing a strong pot of tea to which a big pinch of salt has been added. When the tea is finished it is poured into the tea churn. A hunk of rancid butter is added and the mixture is churned into a thick creamy soup. The nomads are so fond of this tea that the tea churn is one of their most valuable possessions.

Tsamba is eaten with the tea. It is made of roasted barley flour. The flour is glutinous and when it is dipped into the tea it becomes a sticky paste. Even a nomad child can twirl this wad of paste round with his thumb and two fingers to form a ball which he then pops into his mouth. It looks quite easy to do. But just try it for yourself, as many travelers in Tibet have, and you would soon find your hands and face smeared with the gluey dough. You probably wouldn't like its sour taste either.

In the lower altitudes to the east of the Yellow River lie the fields of the Panaka farmers. Men and women in voluminous shubas can be seen working among the rows of barley, which grows well in this altitude where the frost-free season lasts only three months of the year.

If the sun is hot, both men and women slip their arms

out of their shubas and go about naked to the waist. But if a sudden cloud hides the sun, on go the shubas again, for the air without sunlight is very cold.

The villages of the Panakas are made up of adobe houses in the Tibetan style with flat roofs and mere slits for windows to keep out the winter cold. From a distance the villages look as though every woman had her wash out. Scraps of white cloth are fluttering everywhere. They are prayer flags. The Tibetans believe that every time one of the flags waves it is saying a prayer for them.

On the mountain slopes above some of the villages stand ancient lamaseries with thick red walls and gilded roofs. A lamasery is a Tibetan temple and religious center. Communities of priests, or lamas, live there and conduct religious services. But today the number of these lamas has greatly decreased.

After one hundred miles of northward travel, the Yellow River turns east again. Now its way leads through the high desert country of eastern Chinghai. Overhead the sky is a brilliant blue, and the sun beats down harshly. Wherever cultivation is possible there are farmlands. Among them stand clusters of little villages. The houses in these villages have thatched roofs and are the homes of Chinese peasants.

The peasants who live here are very poor. Their blue jackets and trousers are tattered and threadbare. Early in the morning men, women and children leave their villages with hoes over their shoulders, their broad straw hats bobbing along like mushrooms. They are going to spend a long hot day in the fields. Life is difficult for them because as yet they have no modern tools. They must plow, plant, weed, water and harvest by hand. They grow cabbages, potatoes, onions, and beans, but their principal crop is spring wheat. They would much prefer to have rice, but rice needs a great deal of water. Spring wheat, on the other hand, can more easily withstand drought and thrive in poor soil. It also matures before the early winter sets in. Though the Chinghai desert uplands are very hot in summer, they are freezing in the winter.

Here the Yellow River is joined by its first important tributary, the Huangshui, which flows into the Yellow River from the north. A few miles up the Huangshui stands the city of Sining, capital of Chinghai Province.

Sining is an industrial center manufacturing woolen textiles and leather goods and processing dairy products. It looks like any modern factory town that has sprung up quickly. Its shops, apartment buildings and factories are all ugly boxlike structures. Its main streets are paved and are among the widest in the world.

Such handsome streets look strange in Sining because there are scarcely any automobiles to drive along them. Instead the streets are crowded with people. When a driver of the occasional car wants to get through the crowds, he puts his foot on the accelerator and his hand on the horn. The car shoots forward and the honking sends people scattering in all directions.

Off go a group of women in black gowns and cowls. They look like Catholic nuns, but they are Moslem housewives from central Asia. Their husbands wear gray-white pillbox hats. Their faces are swarthy and thickly bearded.

The car sideswipes Tibetans in shubas and felt hats, and Mongolian nomads from the north in handsomely tooled leather boots with turned-up toes. It weaves through hordes of blue-jacketed Chinese, who walk along patiently ignoring the clamor of the horn as long as possible.

If you were riding in that car, you would get a good look at many of the nationalities that make up northern China. Sining, which is centrally located, is the marketplace to which all these people bring their goods for barter.

CHAPTER 2

Moslem Country

About 100 miles below the mouth of the Huangshui, the Yellow River crosses the boundary of Chinghai Province and enters the province of Kansu, which lies to the east. Here it enters a deep gorge, the Liuchia Gorge, where it is hemmed in by 3000-foot-high cliffs.

Once the river rushed along so swiftly through the gorge that it could be crossed at only a few places along the way. At these points barefoot ferrymen, stripped to the waist, waited for passengers. Their ferryboats were made of yak skin stretched over a framework of light wood. Such boats are called coracles.

Recently a dam was built across the mouth of the Liuchia Gorge creating a reservoir. Beyond the dam the river enters open country again. This is the Lanchow Plain. It is almost entirely surrounded by high mountains.

The massive Nan Shan Range crowds down from the northwest. To the east stand the 9000-foot-high Liupan Mountains. To the south tower the 15,000-foot-high Tsinling Mountains, which are a continuation of the Kunlun Range of Tibet and separate the Yellow River from the Yangtze.

The Tsinling Mountains are so high that the moisture-laden monsoon winds blowing up from the south cannot clear them. They drench the Yangtze Valley, leaving the Yellow River Valley semiarid.

Rain averages about fifteen inches a year in Lanchow and falls mainly in the summer. The crops that grow here have to be irrigated. But the soil is fertile, and the river winds among thriving wheat fields and vegetable gardens set out in orderly rows. Occasionally it passes large orchards. In the late summer and early autumn the orchards are colorful with ripening peaches and apricots, pears, apples, and persimmons.

The riverbanks are lined with willow trees and poplars planted years ago. They spread their shade on the turbulent water, which is seven hundred feet wide here and flows along swiftly.

Sometimes, on its way, the river slips by bright blue electric pumps which have been installed along the banks

to siphon out water for irrigation. Young men in blue coveralls tend the pumps. Near each pump is a small thatched shack in which the attendants serving on the night shift can rest.

But there aren't enough electric pumps to irrigate all the fields, so old-fashioned, gigantic waterwheels are used also. Some of the waterwheels are forty feet high. They stand upon the riverbanks revolving like flimsy ferris wheels. Numerous bamboo tubes fastened around the rim dip up water as the wheel carries them through the river. When the tubes reach the top of the wheel, they tilt to pour the water into the fields.

The river is still too swift for boats. It cannot be navigated at all in the winter months because it freezes over. But in late spring and summer and the early fall, it is crowded with rafts.

These rafts are unlike any I have seen in other parts of China. They have to be different because there is no timber or bamboo on the Lanchow Plain out of which to make them. So the rivermen use the only material that is abundant—the whole skins of goats or sheep.

About a dozen of these skins are inflated and fastened together under a framework of branches. The skin rafts are so tough and buoyant that they can carry very heavy loads without bursting or sinking. They are managed by skillful barefoot rivermen in ragged jackets and trousers rolled to the knees.

It looks as though the bouncing rafts will capsize at any moment in the turbulent waters or smash against jutting rocks, or be thrown upon the riverbanks. But always, just in time, the boatman gives a skillful push with his pole and his raft skims out of danger.

Some of the rafts are heaped with vegetables from the fields up-country. Others are stacked with goatskins filled with vegetable oil. Many rafts carry piles of stone and heaps of sand. They are all headed downstream for the city of Lanchow, which stands on the banks of the Yellow River near the center of the plain.

Lanchow is the capital of Kansu Province, and it is an ancient city. In former days it was a caravan stop for the traders who traveled from the West to do business with the Chinese Empire.

China was first opened to land trade from the West by the emperor Han Wu Ti, who ruled from 141 B.C. to 87 B.C. Han Wu Ti sent a powerful army into the Takla Makan Desert, which lies in central Asia. The army conquered all the oasis kingdoms there. This enabled Han Wu Ti to establish a trade route from east to west. Garrisons stationed in the oasis cities could protect the route from the fierce nomads to the north.

The trade route became known as the Silk Road because, in the years that followed, so much silk went out of China over it. Silk went to Persia, Arabia and India, to Turkey

and even to faraway Rome and Egypt. It traveled across the Takla Makan Desert by camel caravan.

Today Lanchow is still an important transportation center, but trains and trucks instead of camels carry the goods. The old city has long since outgrown the earthen walls that once enclosed it. Now it sprawls up and down both sides of the river.

Two bridges connect the divided city. The older one was built in 1910 for road traffic. The second, built in 1954, is a railroad bridge over which the trains rumble on their way to and from central Asia.

Lanchow, like Sining, is a manufacturing town with tanneries and textile mills. Large coal beds nearby provide it with plenty of cheap fuel and the city is building more factories. The rafts that carry sand and stone are bound for the construction sites that line the riverbanks.

At the sites, white-helmeted workers in blue coveralls are riveting, hammering, pouring cement and operating cranes. The crane operators are young people, and a good number of them are girls. Chinese girls, who in the past had to stay at home, are very proud of being allowed to do this kind of work. Many of them are studying to become engineers.

The Yellow River races on—under the bridges and past the city of Lanchow and all the construction sites. It leaves behind the clatter and commotion and soon turns north into the rugged Nan Shan Mountains. Here its way leads through a rocky chasm known as the Chingtung Gorge. Once it rushed furiously along the length of this chasm. But the Chinese have put a stop to that by raising a dam at the far mouth of the gorge, backing up the water and creating another reservoir.

Beyond the dam the river enters level land again. This is the Ningsia Plain. To the west the plain stretches away to the 10,000-foot-high Alashan Mountains, hovering like clouds upon the horizon.

This is still high desert land with about six inches of rainfall a year. Though the soil is fertile, nothing could grow on it if it were not for the Yellow River. It provides the water for the canals which cross the plain. The longest

of these canals, the Hsikan Canal, stretches like a glimmering ribbon from the Yellow River westward to the foothills of the Alashan Mountains some thirty-five miles away.

The canals run in parallel lines, and they also cross each other at right angles. This is done by sending the water of one canal over the other in wooden troughs or cement aqueducts. Rows of willow trees border the canals. Footbridges with bright blue rails cross them at intervals. Peasants on foot or astride mules can be seen passing over the bridges. Sometimes the peasants peddle along on bicycles.

The villages of the Ningsia Plain are prosperous. At night electric lights twinkle from the houses, and here and there you can hear the sound of a radio. Private homes still do not have telephones, but official telephones connect the villages. Electricity has come to the Ningsia Plain as it has to much of China today.

Power poles strung with electric wires march across the wheat fields that roll away to the mountains. Near at hand along the riverbank, peasants work in flooded paddy fields of rice. Rice in northern China is unusual, but the Chinese have been raising it here for centuries. The plain is nicknamed, "South of the Yangtze in the Border Region."

About two million people live on the Ningsia Plain. One third of them are Chinese who follow the Moslem religion. Chinese Moslems are the descendants of Arabian, Turkish and central Asian Moslem traders who came to China centuries ago and settled down here.

The traders married Chinese women and brought their children up in the Moslem faith. To provide these children with Moslem husbands and wives when they grew up, the traders also adopted Chinese babies and reared them as Moslems. The families increased with the years.

Today these Moslems are just about as Chinese as anyone else in China. But because they have a foreign religion, the Chinese Communist government treats them as non-Chinese. The non-Chinese people are considered minorities. They are allowed to keep their own religions and customs. In every other way they are governed the same as all Chinese villages are today.

Each village chooses its own local officials. These officials are experienced farmers. They direct the work of the peasants, who jointly own the fields around their village. The villages sell their produce to state organizations in the city. Some of the money they get is used to pay taxes and to make improvements in the village. Some is divided among the villagers according to the amount of work they have done.

The villages belong to communes. Some communes are small. Others contain as many as twenty-seven villages and nine thousand acres of land. The communes are supervised by trained advisors, or cadres, who are sent by the Communist government in Peking.

The villages contribute funds to the communes to buy tractors, trucks, and threshing machines which are shared by all the villages. Some communes even have small factories which manufacture farm tools. When there is a big job to be done, such as digging a canal or building a dam, the peasants of an entire commune work together on it.

The Moslem Chinese live in their own villages and have their own communes. If you were to stroll through one of their villages, you would soon notice that it is quite different from an ordinary Chinese village.

You wouldn't find a single pig in or around it. Moslems believe that pigs are unclean and the villagers do not eat pork. They don't even like to say the word "pig." They call it "the black one" instead.

Chinese villages have pagodas and old Buddhist temples with paintings on the walls and images behind the altars. Moslem Chinese have small simple churches called mosques. They believe it is wrong to use images or pictures of any kind, and you will find none in their mosques or their homes. However, today in Communist China far fewer people worship either in temples or mosques.

Moslem children are taught the usual subjects of reading, writing, Chinese history, and arithmetic. They also memorize the Arabic alphabet and learn to recite the ancient Moslem prayers in that tongue.

The favorite Moslem holiday is the Feast of Ramadan. It is held at night after a day of fasting. Then whole villages gather for a banquet. If you were traveling the river at that time, you would see the festival fires blazing here and there on the dark plain. You might catch the sound of voices loudly shouting Ramadan greetings to one another.

CHAPTER 3

Beyond the Great Wall

Among the sights to see in the Ningsia Plain are the moldering ruins of an old earthen wall. Much of the wall has been washed away, but here and there sections topped by proud watchtowers still stand.

This wall is the western section of the Great Wall of China. At one time it stretched unbroken for fifteen hundred miles from the sea in the east across the northern boundary of China to the deserts in the west. It was built in 210 B.C. by China's first historic emperor, Chin Shih Huang Ti. Chin Shih Huang Ti sentenced millions of his subjects to work on the wall. It was his favorite form of punishment for all those who offended him. The life of these prisoners was so hard that tens of thousands of them died before the wall was completed.

The wall was to serve as a defense against the fierce nomad tribes to the north of China. During Chin Shih Huang Ti's day these tribes were unified under a single leader named Touman. They were known as the Hsiung-nu. They lived in felt tents called yurts and roamed the wide steppes with their flocks of sheep and herds of cattle and horses.

The Hsiung-nu were jealous of the rich country to the south. They called China the Great Diamond, because her fertile lands were more highly valued by them than precious stones. Often they conducted raids upon the Chinese farms near their borders. They would pillage the villages, kill the men, take the women and children captive and drive off all the livestock.

Chin Shih Huang Ti's massive wall was set with watchtowers at intervals of a third of a mile. Sentries in the towers kept constant watch on the steppelands beyond. They would report any warlike concentration of nomads. Then the Chinese troops would be called up to man that section of the wall. With their powerful crossbows they could drive back the Mongols who possessed only lighter bows.

In the centuries that followed, the power of the Hsiung-nu faded, but other fierce nomad kingdoms rose to take their place. The Great Wall was a good defense against these nomad warriors only if the ruler of China was strong. If he was weak, he was careless about maintaining soldiers along the wall. If he was troubled with civil war, he didn't have enough men to spare for it.

Then the tribes from the north had no difficulty breaching the wall and swarming down into northern China. Some of the tribal leaders allowed their men to massacre the Chinese peasants and turn the farmlands into pasturage for their herds of sheep and cattle. Others became emperors, ruling in the Chinese way with fixed courts and civil laws instead of tribal ones. The greatest of these emperors was the Mongol Kublai Khan, who established his capital at Peking and ruled there from 1264 to 1294.

Today Mongolia is divided in half. The northern half is called Outer Mongolia and has an independent government. The southern half, which is separated from the

northern by the barren Gobi Desert, is called Inner Mongolia. It is united with China, and the Mongolians who live there are treated as a minority people.

After the Yellow River passes by the ruins of the wall, it continues on for three hundred miles. Then it takes an eastern course for two hundred miles, after which it turns south again. This loop is known as the Great Bend.

The river flows lazily on its course northward, greeted now and then by the whistle of a train traveling along its western bank. Presently the cultivated lands to the west give way to the wastes of the Alashan Desert, which is an extension of the Gobi. To the east the equally barren Ordos Desert slopes up in a jumble of red cliffs and broken highlands.

The southern boundary of the Ordos is the low Paiyu Range over which the Great Wall proudly marches. Its other three boundaries are formed by the encircling river.

At the eastward bend of the river a little town of red brick buildings stands on the outer shore. This is the Mongolian town of Bayingol. Beyond Bayingol the river flows passed a broad cultivated plain. It is called the Outer Bend Plain.

In times of heavy rain the river used to overflow its low banks here and destroy the crops. It can't do so now because the peasants have built up the riverbanks with earthen walls, or dikes. There is a new dam, too, near Bayingol. Ten large canals and many smaller ones lace the plain and turn it into a giant checkerboard of growing wheat.

Beyond the plain to the north lie the steppes, covered with straw-yellow grass that sometimes grows as tall as a man on horseback. Out there Mongolian herdsmen tend thousands of head of cattle and sheep.

In late fall the river is alive with noisy ducks and geese traveling south in wavering black lines that stretch from horizon to horizon. The birds are escaping the winter gales which will soon be blowing down from the Arctic.

The gales are called the Yellow Winds because they are laden with river silt and fine sand from the Gobi Desert to the north of the steppelands. When the winds are blowing, a golden haze covers the sky. If they should last for

several days the air becomes thick and gloomy. You would find it difficult to breathe, and your throat and mouth would feel dry and dusty. When the winds finally stop blowing, there is a thick layer of sand and silt spread over everything in sight—fields, pasturelands, river, canals, and roads.

The action of the Yellow Winds over the centuries has heaped giant sand dunes along the course of the Yellow River. Dunes stretch across the western boundary of the cultivated Outer Bend Plain. Almost twenty years ago the peasants of the region began planting a row of fast-growing desert trees in front of the dunes. Today a wall of living green screens their fields from the dunes and the drifting sands of the neighboring Alashan Desert.

In winter the Alashan Mountains are capped with snow, but little moisture falls along the Great Bend because the air is so dry. The weather, however, is very cold, and the peasants put on layer upon layer of padded blue clothing to keep warm.

They light fires under the kangs in their homes. A kang is a large brick platform two to three feet high which serves as the family bedstead. The platform contains a flue into which fuel is stuffed and lighted.

In many homes the fuel will be coal because there are rich coalfields nearby. The people of China have used coal for centuries. The Italian March Polo, who lived at the court of Kublai Khan from 1275 to 1292, returned home to describe the strange black rocks that the Chinese burned for heat. Everyone thought he was a liar or just mad.

If coal isn't available for the kangs, dry twigs, reeds, and even cattle dung are used. This kind of fuel burns quickly, often with a great deal of smoke. Once the kang is heated, the bricks of which it is made keep warm for a long time. Sometimes the bricks become overheated and then people may get burned.

In the coldest weather the children keep warm by playing on top of the kangs. Of course, they have fun outdoors, too. They have never heard of skates, but after the river freezes over they have just as much fun sliding across the ice on their soft cloth shoes or the seat of their padded trousers.

When the spring thaws melt the ice, the Yellow River comes to life again. Skin rafts, large flat-bottomed barges, and even motor tugs make their way up and down the stream transporting grains, vegetables, and sacks of salt to the towns and cities upon the riverbank.

The salt is quarried from the shores of drying salt lakes in the Takla Makan and Gobi deserts. It has to be brought by camel caravan to the river. There may be as many as a hundred camels in one caravan, each one bearing a load of six hundred pounds. Five or six camel drivers herd the long procession across the desert.

The camel drivers camp on the banks of the river to unload their salt. They are tall dark Mongolians or central Asians with leathery faces seamed with wrinkles. They wear long greasy sheepskin coats, thick rawhide boots, and turbans wound round their heads.

Much of the salt goes downstream by barge to the city of Paotow, which stands on the northern shore of the Great Bend.

For years Paotow was a simple trading center standing on the Mongolian side of the boundary between China and Mongolia. Here Mongolian herdsmen from the steppes brought their raw wool and hide and bartered for necessities. At that time Paotow was a little fortress town enclosed by high earthen walls. The houses were small adobe buildings. Numerous pagodas pierced the sky with their spires.

Today rich deposits of coal and iron ore in the Mongolian steppes nearby have turned Paotow into one of the five largest steel-producing centers in China. Its population has jumped from 90,000 to 2,000,000 people.

The first steel mill at Paotow was built after the Communist Chinese came to power in 1952. Russia helped the new government with the mill by lending money, technicians, and equipment.

When the mill was finished, it covered five square miles and bristled with smokestacks. It began producing in 1960.

Today workers in white caps and coveralls turn out a million tons of steel a year.

Many other factories have been built since the first steel mill went into operation. They line a five-mile length of paved road that runs along the north shore of the Yellow River. There are factories that produce railroad equipment, heavy machinery, power tools, and building materials. There are large packing centers that process beef and mutton for export, and textile mills that weave woolen fabrics. More factories are being built, and with them apartment buildings, schools, opera houses, and hospitals.

Hundreds of people pour into Paotow to work in the factories. They come on foot and by the train which passes through Paotow on its way east to the capital at Peking or west to Lanchow in Kansu Province. They sit packed together on the wooden benches in the third-class compartments of the train, rumbling along to a new life in a frontier town.

Chinese come from the south and Mongolians from the north. In the city of Paotow you can't tell one nationality from the other, because the Mongolians, who look very much like Chinese, have discarded their traditional dress. Instead of long nomad robes bound at the waist with a girdle, baggy breeches, and boots with turned-up toes, they dress in blue jackets and trousers.

Construction gangs can't keep up with the crowds of

newcomers. There are never enough apartment buildings. People have to live in tents until there is room for them. Tents surround every factory.

The two million people of Paotow have to eat, so more and more farmlands are being carved out of the grazing lands behind Paotow and sowed to wheat. Food also comes by train, and it comes by the Yellow River. Rafts, barges, and tugs line the riverfront. Jostling, shouting porters unload the boats and pack the produce in huge wicker baskets. Up the bank and into the city the porters swarm with the heavy baskets swinging from carrying poles across their shoulders—food for the people of Paotow.

on their way to the Yellow River. It was along the banks of the rivers that Chinese civilization began. The rivers provided water for irrigation, and the loess hills and cliff sides could be used for cave homes. Such homes are easy to dig because loess is soft. But it also adheres firmly together. The homes can be used for as long as thirty years before there is any danger of cave-in.

As the farmers increased in number, they needed more

land. They began terracing the hills and tilling them. Then they climbed the mountains, which were thickly forested, and cleared more plots. Bit by bit as the centuries went by, the farmers cut down the great forests. Finally they were all gone. Naked mountains looked down on the Great Loess.

There is very little rainfall on the Great Loess, usually less than thirteen inches a year. It falls in the summertime, sometimes in torrents. With all the forest cover gone, the water rushes unchecked down the slopes of the mountains and the hills, washing away fields and destroying the young crops.

At other times there were droughts when scarcely any rain at all fell. Even the Yellow River dwindled away and the crops withered. In spite of its rich soil, the Great Loess became one of the poorest spots in the world. Famines were frequent. People ate grass, leaves, and clay, trying to keep alive. Millions died. In the famine years, buyers would appear in the Great Loess. They had come to purchase children from starving families to sell as slaves in the eastern cities.

The other nations of the world used to send large contributions to the famine-stricken areas of China because China could do little to help her starving people. After 1911, when the last emperor of the Ching Dynasty was overthrown and China became a republic, she was torn by Civil War. Then in 1937 the Japanese invaded her territory, and for eight years she struggled against her old enemy. This was the time of World War II which ended with Japan's defeat. But it did not bring peace to China. The Civil War continued between the Nationalist Party under Chiang Kai-shek and the Communist Party under Mao Tse-tung.

Finally in 1949 the Communist government came to power in China. By this time China was so impoverished that she had little modern equipment of any kind. But there were plenty of people, 825 million of them. Everything depended on what these millions of people could do without machinery to help them.

The farmers of the Great Loess realized that if they built dams across the mouths of the ravines they could keep their fields from being washed away and save the water that was now being wasted. They had no time to work on these dams during the growing season. But after the fall harvests were in, the villages organized work brigades.

Men, women, and older children all joined the brigades. From the mountainsides they dug out rocks with spades and picks. In long plodding files they trudged down to the dam sites carrying heavy loads of rock slung from poles over their shoulders. They worked through the freezing winter in their tattered clothes and bare feet. But slowly, rock by rock, the dams went up all over the Great Loess.

Other work was going on, too. The villagers cut out highways for trucks and buses and laid railroad tracks, doing it all by hand. In the old days it took a long time to travel through the Great Loess. You either went astride a mule or in a cart drawn by one. Today you can travel by train or bus, or even fly by plane from Peking.

From the plane windows you can see the brown thread of the Yellow River and the reservoirs scattered through the Great Loess. The reservoirs not only provide water for irrigation, they are also stocked with fish. The peasants of Shensi, who never tasted fish before, are enjoying it today.

In the spring the hills and valleys are green with wheat and vegetables. The hilltops are crowned with dark clumps of pine trees and fruit-bearing orchards which were planted by the villagers when they changed the face of the Great Loess. You don't see villages from the air, for most of the peasants of the Great Loess still live in cave homes. These homes are warm in winter and cool in summer, and most of the loess people find them more comfortable than adobe huts.

One of these cave villages is called Liu Ling, which

means Willow Grove, and it is located on the Yenan River, a small tributary of the Yellow River.

About two hundred people live in Liu Ling. Their cave homes are dug into the hillside, one above the other. Every home is equipped with a wooden door and a window covered with thin paper instead of glass. Winding paths lead to the cave homes on the upper slopes.

The people of Liu Ling are still poor; but they no longer fear famine, and they have many more possessions than in the past. A few of them own bicycles, and most of them have extra quilts. Many of the caves have electric lighting. And though the villagers still cannot afford radios, they can have a loudspeaker installed in their homes for a few

cents a year. Music and news broadcasts are piped into the loudspeakers from a central radio.

The peasants of Liu Ling are trying something new on their land. They are growing rice in the valley. The reservoirs that enable them to flood low-lying lands make this possible. Up on the terraced hill slopes, millet, corn, wheat, and giant melons grow.

If you were passing the melon fields at night during the ripening season, you might hear the strains of a Chinese flute. It is the night watchman sitting in his little thatched lean-to, playing music to drive away the sly thieving foxes.

On the brush-covered hills beyond the cultivated land, flocks of sheep, goats, and cattle graze under the care of village herdsmen. But pigs and chickens are sheltered in fenced-in caves because no one wants to waste open land on them. Periodically the animals are slaughtered, and the carcasses are hauled away to be sold at a packing plant in northern Shensi. From the packing plant tinned meat goes out to eastern Europe.

In China today, though the villagers share their farm lands, individual peasants still own small private gardens and a few domestic animals. Such is the case in Liu Ling even though it is a poor village. Men and women too old for work in the fields weed and water the family vegetable garden. You will see the old women having difficulty walking. If you look at their feet, you will find they are no larger than goat hoofs.

When these women were young, it was considered fashionable for women to have small feet. A girl with large feet couldn't get a husband. So at the age of eight, almost every girl in China had her feet bound. They were wrapped in tough strips of cloth which were soaked in water to make them shrink. Every day the strips were pulled tighter. It was so painful that the little girls often cried for days at a time. After five to seven years, the binding was removed. The girls were crippled for life and could only hobble along. But their parents had no trouble finding husbands for them.

Today footbinding is against the law, and girls are as free as boys. They attend school and receive an equal education. Though schooling is not compulsory in China, ninety percent of the children go because their parents want them to have a good education.

There is a primary school for every five villages in the Great Loess. Liu Ling has one of these schools, which is attended by more than 180 pupils. They are taught by ten teachers and a principal.

The schoolrooms are large caves at ground level. The schoolyard is the open space in front of the caves. A Chinese schoolyard is quite colorful because the parents love to dress their children in gay clothes. All the little girls wear flowered jackets and bright ribbons in their hair.

The school day starts with the children being inspected for cleanliness. The teachers check the younger children.

The older children check one another. Neck? Fingernails? Ears? This is something new for the people who live in the Great Loess.

In the old days when there was no water for much of the year, no one took baths. Today there is water enough in the reservoirs for everyone. And because it is very hard to keep clean in the Great Loess, many of the children get two baths a day. Since soap is scarce, the children are sometimes scoured with sand.

Besides their regular studies, the children of Liu Ling learn how to grow vegetables. They have their own school plot and plant pumpkins, tomatoes, and corn. No one is forced to work in the garden. Volunteers do everything.

When the vegetables are ripe, the school cook sells them

in the town of Yenan, which is a few miles to the north on the Yenan River. He comes back with delicacies he has bought and prepares a big feast to which all the children are invited.

Sometimes the whole school pays a visit to Yenan, which has many museums and historic places of interest for the Communist Chinese. It is the birthplace of today's Chinese Communist government. Here in 1936 Mao Tse-tung came with the remnants of his tattered army. He was in flight from Chiang Kai-shek and his much stronger Nationalist army.

Mao Tse-tung lived in Yenan while he organized the Communist Party and conducted guerrilla warfare, both against the Nationalists and the Japanese. Every tourist who goes to Yenan visits the cave home in which Mao Tse-tung stayed while he made plans for the day when China would be united under Communist rule.

Today Mao Tse-tung is able to put those plans into operation. As Chairman Mao of the Chinese Communist Party, he is the most powerful man in China.

CHAPTER 5

The San Men Dam

During its course from north to south, the Yellow River gathers the water of many small tributaries and two large ones. The first of these large tributaries is the Fen Ho. Its source lies in the northern mountains of the Taihang Range. And it flows southwestward along the eastern foot of the Luliang Mountains to join the Yellow River about seventy-five miles north of the place where it makes a final bend eastward.

The second large tributary is the Wei. It flows along the northern foot of the Tsinling Range to enter the Yellow River at the final bend itself.

Since all these tributaries, large and small, pass through loess, they bring a tremendous amount of sediment to the

Yellow River. The sediment is especially heavy during flood stages. At these times the river often carries up to 40 percent silt. Sometimes it may be as high as 48 percent. Other large rivers seldom carry more than 2 or 3 percent silt even at floodtime. Imagine a river which is almost half mud!

On its journey eastward, the rich muddy water of the Yellow River used to boil through a steep gorge between a series of cliffs and bluffs, a thousand to three thousand feet high. The gorge is known as the San Men Gorge. San Men means Three Gates. The name was given to the gorge because formerly its mouth was broken by two rock islands which separated the river into three narrows. The first narrows was called Gate of Man, the second Gate of the Gods, and the third Gate of the Dragon. But all the gates have now disappeared under a huge dam which was finished in 1960.

The building of the San Men Dam was a great event for the simple peasants who live here. Their cave homes pockmark the cliffs and bluffs that line the river, and their fields lie on the loess plateau above.

None of the peasants had ever seen motor-operated equipment before. They traveled by cart and mule and used primitive spades and hoes and even wooden plows to till their land.

Then things began to change. It started in the ancient

village of Hui Hsin which is near the site chosen for the dam. First railroad tracks were rerouted to touch at Hui Hsin. Then freight cars began to rumble in, bringing giant machines and modern tools—cranes, tractors, motor tugs, riveting machines, and blowtorches. Some of this equipment had come from Russia and Europe. But a great deal of it had been manufactured in new Chinese factories.

The first personnel to arrive were the engineers. A modern hotel went up to house them. Brick apartment buildings followed for the workers who started pouring in. Twenty-one thousand of them came. Two thousand were women.

The night before work began, the labor gangs gathered

on the bluff above the river to hold a long torchlight procession and make a vow to tame the river. The old peasants who lived in the region were very troubled. For years they had suffered from the flooding of the Yellow River. They believed that it was caused by a Dragon God who lived there, and they tried to keep him contented by worshipping with incense and prayers and offerings of pigs, sheep, and horses. Even the powerful first emperor, Chin Shih Huang Ti, who had built the Great Wall, had been afraid of the Dragon God's anger.

Once a year Chin Shih Huang Ti offered the god the most beautfiul girl in the empire as a bride. The girl was dressed in a rich bridal costume and given a fine feast. Then she was sent whirling down the river on a light raft. When she disappeared, it was believed the Dragon God had come for her and put her in his palace along with all the other beautiful brides.

Now the peasants were sure that the labor gangs would ruin the Dragon God's home and make him angry enough to destroy them all. They watched gloomily as workers in white hoods and capes to protect themselves from flying debris began dynamiting rocks from the cliffs along the riverbanks. Tractors rumbled up and down the steep slopes. Giant cranes, operated by young men and women, deposited steel and concrete beams where they were needed. Steel girders went up.

Thousands of workers in helmets, dungarees, and heavy boots mixed and poured concrete under the direction of the engineers. Step by step a barrier of rock was laid across the Yellow River. It rose until it stood 350 feet high, a massive man-made mountain, broken by a dozen spillways each equipped with two gates. Overhead sluice gate-controls weighing 250 tons regulated the flow of water through the spillways into the lower bed of the Yellow River.

When the Yellow River reached this new barrier, it was forced to drop its load of silt. Just above and below the dam it lost its usual muddy color and became clear and blue. The old peasants said it was a miracle.

Behind the dam the waters of the Wei, the largest tributary of the Yellow River, began to back up to form a reservoir 194 miles long. This reservoir is larger than the American Grand Coulee and Boulder Dam reservoirs combined. It has become China's second largest lake.

Of course, the reservoir caused many changes in the valley of the Wei. Half a million people whose fields lay in its path had to be moved. Some of them were given land elsewhere. Others found jobs in the new industries and towns that sprang up along the shores of the new lake.

A trip by motorboat up this lake begins at the first town ever to be built on its shores. The town is called Ta An, which means Great Peace, and is occupied by dam personnel. It stands under towering bluffs pocked with the cave homes of about six thousand peasants.

Twenty-seven thousand people live in the tile-roofed bungalows of Ta An. They have schools, a shopping center, and a theater. The river provides them with electricity and telephone service. Even the peasants in their cave homes have electricity now. They are no longer afraid of the Yellow River. Their children have learned to drive trucks and work drills and do other construction work. Many of them are ambitious to go to school and learn more of this new way of life.

There are boats of all kinds on the lake. Some are motor ferries and others are fishing junks. The reservoir has been stocked with fish, and there are small canneries along the shore. Fishermen in straw hats or turbans, and trousers rolled to the knee, unload their catch at the piers that jut out from the canneries. Porters with baskets over their shoulders carry the fish into the canneries, where it is processed and tinned for sale in the big cities of Europe.

Now and then as you continue up the lake you will come to noisy boatyards. Carpenters in blue jackets and trousers using hammers and saws are working on the half-finished hulls of boats for lake and river use.

At the head of the reservoir, the motor tugs can enter the Wei River and travel to Sian a short distance upstream. All along the way the riverbanks are lined with factories. Beyond them fields of cotton stretch to the craggy slopes of the Tsinling Mountains. Sian itself, once an ancient capital, is a bustling textile center which turns out millions of yards of cotton cloth every year.

China's second ancient capital lies to the east of the San Men Dam. It is named Loyang and is more than three thousand years old. To reach Loyang you have to go back down the Wei River and through the reservoir again. Then your motorboat goes through a canal blasted in solid rock to bypass the great dam.

Once through the canal, you will be on the Yellow River again, slipping by the still-growing town of Hui Hsin, now renamed San Men City. About seventy-five miles farther is the little tributary called the Lo, which flows northward into the Yellow River. Loyang stands on this tributary just a few miles south of the Yellow River.

If you were to visit Loyang you would surely be taken to the cave temples of Lungmen, about sixteen miles south of the city. The temples date from the seventh century and were hollowed out of the cliffs that line the small Yi River. Standing in these caves are thousands of statues and statuettes of Gautama Buddha, a great Indian teacher who lived in the sixth century B.C. Buddha founded the Buddhist religion which spread from India through central Asia and into China.

The statues were carved out of the soft sandstone walls of the caves themselves. The largest statue stands fifty feet high. The smallest is only eight inches tall.

The carving of the cave temples, together with all the statuary, bas reliefs, and inscriptions that decorate them, was ordered by the first empress to rule China, the cruel Wu Tzu-tien of the Tang Dynasty. Empress Wu Tzu-tien held court in Loyang, which today is made up of two sections. One is the old town with narrow winding streets surrounded by earthen walls. The other section is modern Loyang. Large deposits of iron and coal nearby have turned the ancient city into a modern industrial center. China's largest tractor plant is located in the suburbs of Loyang. It is called Tractor Plant No. 1, and it was built with the help of Russian equipment and engineers.

For several years Russian engineers stayed to give advice; but in 1960 the governments of China and Russia quarreled, and the Russians were called home. Today everything is run by the Chinese.

Tractor Plant No. 1 is like a small city with wide paved streets, sidewalks, and shopping centers. One hundred thousand people live here. Twenty-three hundred of them work in the plant. Their children go to school in new brick buildings.

Besides their regular studies, the children have workshops where they spend two hours a week, making furniture and pottery, or learning how to assemble small table radios. If you were to visit one of these workshop classes it would remind you of the manual arts courses in your local high

school. But instead of taking home what they make, the children of the Tractor Plant No. 1 school sell their products and put the proceeds into a school welfare fund.

The families of Tractor Plant No. 1 live in rows of new brick apartment buildings. You and I would find the apartments very cramped. But though the living rooms are tiny, they are neatly kept with curtains at the windows and pictures on the walls. They are simply furnished with a table, several chairs, and usually a small radio.

There are also apartments with an extra bedroom, a private shower, and a kitchen. But these rooms are just cubbyholes. The apartments are lighted with electricity and have running water and steam heat, which are all free. Cooking is done on coal bricks which are bought in the marketplace.

The wages of the workers at Tractor Plant No. 1 are low. They earn between twenty to thirty dollars a month. But rent is low too—about a dollar a month. The workers get benefits such as free medical service for themselves and at half price for their dependents.

Since both husbands and wives usually work, many of the employees at Tractor Plant No. 1 prefer to take their families to evening meals in the factory canteen. The food is prepared by cooks paid from factory funds, and there are some forty hot dishes on the menu to choose from.

In the large dining hall, the families share tables with one another, and there is a friendly chatter of voices and clatter of chopsticks as the meal progresses. Five cents in the canteen will buy a big bowl of rice and a bowl of vegetables and meat. Dessert—cake or ice cream—costs two cents extra. Afterward, for entertainment, the families may go to the theater to see a movie, or they may just stroll along the street visiting with friends.

CHAPTER 6

The Flood

Beyond Loyang the Yellow River leaves the loess high-lands at a little town called Mengtsin. Here it enters the province of Honan, which straddles the Yellow River to the east of Shansi Province. It now has 478 miles more to travel before it reaches the Gulf of Po Hai to the east. Its course leads through a broad sloping plain which at Mengtsin has an elevation of only 397 feet above sea level.

This plain was created by the Yellow River and several other smaller rivers. Millions of years ago the rivers plunged from the highlands right into the ocean. But the ocean offshore was shallow, and the rivers poured tons of silt into this area from the Great Loess. The silt filled up 125,000 square miles with fertile earth. This is now known as the North China Plain.

The North China Plain includes three provinces: Hopei, which contains the capital of Peking, Honan, and Shantung.

When early man began to cultivate the North China Plain he had to build dikes on either side of the Yellow River to protect his fields from flooding. There were no rocks to speak of on the plain, so the peasants had to build mud dikes. Since these dikes were not strong enough to take the full force of the river when it was in flood, the peasants placed the dikes several miles apart. This allowed the river to meander as it pleased over a wide bed.

Before the San Men Dam was built, the yearly load of silt the Yellow River brought to the North China Plain was thirty-five billion cubic feet. Each year the river deposited twenty billion cubic feet of this silt in its bed on its way to the sea. If you were to spread these twenty billion cubic feet of silt out, they would cover seven hundred square miles with one foot of silt. As you can see, this is a lot of silt.

The silt kept raising the bed of the river, and the peasants kept raising the dikes to keep out the water. Now they look like parallel ranges of low hills. The dikes are so old that you can find coins embedded in them that came from the Han Dynasty, which ruled China from 206 B.C. to A.D. 220.

If the summer rains are heavy, there is always danger from a breach at a weak point in the dikes. The water rushing through the breach will quickly wear it into a mile-wide gap and the plain will be flooded.

So at low-water times, groups of men directed by engineers inspect the dikes for flaws and repair them. It may be a hair's-breadth crack caused by the baking sun. It may be a rat tunnel, or the burrow of a fox. There are not many foxes left on the plain. The Chinese have organized a trapping program that has eliminated almost all of them. A single fox burrow can mean the difference between life and death for millions of people.

Along the most exposed sections of the dikes, hundreds of men face the mud walls with blocks of white stone, which they chisel and cut into shape. The stone is quarried

in distant mountains and brought by trucks and trains. The government in China is making every effort to keep the Yellow River within its dikes.

No other river in the world threatens the people who live on its banks with such constant danger. Through the centuries floods and droughts have occurred so frequently along its course that an old Chinese proverb says, "Of every ten seasons, nine are disastrous." It is no wonder that the Chinese call the Yellow River "China's Sorrow."

The worst Yellow River flood in modern history occurred in 1938 near Chengchow, capital of Honan Province, which stands near the dikes of the Yellow River about fifty miles from Loyang. The flood was man-made, and its purpose was to stop the advance of the Japanese army. The Nationalist government then ruling China blew up the dikes near Chengchow to keep the Japanese from reaching Hankow on the Yangtze River to the south.

The Yellow River floods poured out over much of Honan, turning six million acres of cultivated land into a sea of mud. Fields and villages were inundated. Thousands of people were drowned. As the mud dried, the land was turned into a desert where no food of any kind could be found. The flood was followed by famine. Eight hundred and eighty thousand people died, and six million more were made homeless.

During the years that followed, the Yellow River continued to flow southward over Honan. Since it had no channel, it meandered across country in a yellow-brown coil of water that kept changing course. Two million acres of land could not be cultivated because of the wandering river.

In 1945, after the war with Japan was over, the United Nations offered to aid Nationalist China in returning the river to its old course. The Civil War was still going on, and Nationalist and Communist forces were battling in Honan Province where the work had to be done. But both sides were so eager to get the Yellow River back into its bed that they made a pact to stay on opposite sides of the river until the repairs were completed.

In 1947 after two years of work, the new dike was finished. The thousands of workmen went home, and the Civil War began again along that stretch of river.

CHAPTER 7

From Chengchow to the Sea

Chengchow, where the river dikes were breached in 1938, was once a dingy ancient town, but today it is an important textile center and has been almost entirely rebuilt. New yellow brick apartment buildings face wide streets lined with shade trees. There are spacious parkways on either side of the main streets and an esplanade runs down their center.

Beyond Chengchow the fertile plain stretches away on all sides. It is dotted with ponds and seamed with canals. The largest of these canals is the thirty-mile-long People's Victory Canal which was finished in 1953. It connects the Yellow River with a shallow river, also called the Wei, which flows northward. The water brought from the Yel-

low River to the Wei enables one-hundred-ton junks to navigate it.

Early travelers along the Yellow River paying it another visit today find a great difference in the landscape. Once the surrounding plain was almost bare of trees, but in recent years the Chinese have been conducting a gigantic reforestation program. Now there are many orchards and copses of dark-green shade trees scattered over the countryside.

Here and there villages of small adobe houses with thatched roofs cluster under the trees. The villages are so close together that no matter where you go you will never be out of sight of one or more of them. More people live on the North China Plain than in any other section of

China, and perhaps even the world. One sixth of China's population is crowded together here.

Rainfall on the plain averages twenty inches a year and turns the land into yellow mud. Then from horizon to horizon you will see blue-coated farmers preparing their fields for sowing. Tractors, driven by young technicians, creep along like gigantic beetles drawing straight furrows behind them. But there aren't enough tractors yet for every farmer. So peasants plod through the mud behind steel plows harnessed to mules or even to teams of other human beings.

By midsummer the sea of yellow mud has turned into a sea of growing things. The riverbanks are lined with fields of peanut bushes flaunting their yellow pea-shaped blooms. Beyond are fields of light-green wheat and others of dark-green tobacco. This is also cotton country, and there are almost as many fields of cotton as of wheat. There are many kinds of vegetables grown here. Between the rows of young corn, beans, pumpkins, and tomatoes walk young girls wearing masks, spraying insecticides from large tanks slung from their shoulders.

Not even the land beyond the reach of water is wasted. Here you will find fields of dark-green kaoliang. Kaoliang is a species of broomcorn and looks somewhat like corn. But its leaves are much coarser, and it bears no ears. It grows eight to ten feet high and is topped by a tassel of kernels, each the size of a small pea.

Kaoliang is a very popular crop in northern China because it can withstand drought and supply food when other crops fail. But it is not very tasty and is normally used for cattle feed.

Every commune on the plain owns large herds of cattle and flocks of sheep and goats. Tended by sunburned herdsmen, they graze on lands where cultivation is impossible.

A few miles beyond Chengchow the Yellow River passes under a new double-track railroad bridge. Because the dikes are so far apart, it is one of the longest bridges in the world. Trains clatter over it on their way to and from Peking in the north and Nanking in the south. In the daytime the tracks gleam like a silver ribbon above the river. After dark, a shaft of light from every passing engine is thrown upon the roiling brown waters below.

Sixty miles from Chengchow the Yellow River arrives at the little town of Kaifeng. Kaifeng was once the capital of China. Then it became the capital of Honan Province. But constant threat of flooding in this low-lying area caused the Chinese to move their capital to Chengchow.

With every mile eastward the river's bed has been widening, until at Kaifeng the parallel dikes are thirteen miles apart. Danger of flooding has always been greatest at low-lying Kaifeng. From this point the Yellow River has changed course repeatedly, now flowing north, now south, very much like the wagging tail of a friendly dog. Each time it shifts course it deposits billions of cubic feet of silt over a wide area. It is this silt that makes up the plain of Shantung Province lying to the east of Honan.

Shantung Province is a peninsula, the farthest tip of which is mountainous. Millions of years ago these mountains were offshore islands. Now Yellow River silt binds them to the mainland.

Today the Yellow River flows northeast through this plain and, after a journey of another three hundred miles, enters the Gulf of Po Hai. The slope of the land toward the sea is so gentle that the river is forced to drop more and more of its burden of silt. It has dropped so much that it now flows on a ridge across Shantung to the sea. The river bed is more than a mile wide here and is hemmed in by towering dikes which are forty-three feet high in some places. The dikes are entirely faced with stone or brick. A parallel row of dikes set a mile or so from the first gives added protection to the people of Shantung.

The river is extremely dangerous in Shantung because of its high bed. When the river is full, the water may be twenty-five feet above the surrounding plain. Since the plain slopes away from the dikes, the water would rush downhill for miles if it were to break loose.

The Shantung peninsula averages thirty inches of rain a year, most of it in the summer. If the rain comes in torrents, the Yellow River quickly reaches flood stage. Choppy with waves, it goes rushing along tearing at its banks.

There have been no serious floods in Shantung in recent years. But in 1958 during a period of especially heavy rains the Yellow River began to break through its dikes in a number of places. A million peasants were mobilized to seal the breaches before any serious damage was done.

There is considerable river traffic on the lower course of the Yellow River. Convoys of fishing boats with sun-blackened fishermen let down nets into the brown river waters to haul up catches of carp. Stately transport junks with brown sails pass by, along with squat barges carrying grain, tractors, trucks, cement, stone, and steel pipes. Now and then a trim little motor tug takes off from a small jetty with a load of passengers bound for the opposite shore.

A little more than a hundred miles from Kaifeng, the river traffic travels at right angles as well as up and down stream. Here the Yellow River is cut by a large canal. This is the Grand Canal, or Grand Transport River, as the Chinese call it, and is one of the man-made wonders of the world.

The Grand Canal was built piecemeal over a number of centuries. Every time an emperor changed his capital to a different location, he extended the Grand Canal to it so that supplies could be brought to his court. At last the Grand Canal reached a length of 1286 miles. It stretched

from Hangchow on the Chientang River south of the Yangtze, through Tientsin to Peking some two hundred and fifty miles north of the Yellow River.

Like the Yellow River, the Grand Canal has to cross Shantung Province on a ridge enclosed in dikes. It is still the longest canal in the world and is the only waterway in China that runs north and south. In the nineteenth century it was neglected. Silt and debris were allowed to clog the northern sections making them unnavigable.

The Chinese are now repairing and enlarging the canal along its whole length. Today, as in Kublai Khan's time, you can see loaded barges crisscrossing the Yellow River on their way up or down the ancient waterway.

As the river flows eastward from the Grand Canal, the tented blue slopes of Tai Shan rise abruptly out of the plain. The ancient Chinese believed Tai Shan was the most sacred mountain in the world. Emperors used to make yearly visits to it to conduct solemn rites on its summit.

Today Tai Shan is visited by many tourists, who climb the six thousand steps to the top for the fine view. They also like to visit the town of Chufu, which stands at the base of Tai Shan. Confucius, China's most famous sage, was born here in 551 B.C. A splendid temple stands there in his honor. His grave, marked by a simple stone tablet, lies in an ancient graveyard under spreading trees.

In the shadow of Tai Shan and just a little to the south

of the river stands the ancient city of Tsinan, the capital of Shantung Province. Surrounded by cotton fields, Tsinan has been a textile center for many years. However, because of plentiful deposits of coal and iron nearby, it has recently mushroomed into a large industrial city, manufacturing Diesel engines and machine tools.

Like most Chinese cities today, Tsinan is made up of two sections. In the old section you would find yourself walking through narrow lanes bordered by walled-in courtyards. Occasionally you would chance upon a little shrine or a canal where women come to wash their clothes. In other canals—there are many in Tsinan—workmen go fishing for their dinner in their free time. Even when it is raining, you would always find a fisherman or two squatting on the bank of a canal. Huddled under his bulky straw raincape and hat, he waits patiently for the fish to bite.

Almost everywhere you go in old Tsinan you would come upon a spring surrounded by a little park where children play after school. Tsinan has so many of these springs that it is known as the City of Springs. The streams flowing from the springs join to form a pretty little lake in the center of the city.

Here ferrymen wait in canopied boats to take tourists on pleasure rides around the lake. Along its shore, where big blue lotus lilies grow thickly, men gather lotus roots, which make good eating. With their toes they grope around in

the thick mud for the roots and then pull them up with a jerk. The men wear single huge lotus leaves wrapped round their heads like a bandana. Lotus leaf shawls over their shoulders protect them from sun and rain alike. They bundle their roots in lotus leaf wrappings before taking them to market.

The new section of Tsinan gives you the feeling of being in an altogether different city. Here crowds of energetic workers pour in and out of factories. Whistles blow. Smokestacks belch black smoke. Down the wide streets lined with new apartment buildings you hear the clang of trolleys and the honking of buses. An occasional truck, or a crane headed for a new construction site, goes rumbling by.

But everything in industrial Tsinan isn't run the modern way. Most of the transportation of materials is still done on foot. Thousands of porters trudge the streets harnessed to carts loaded with all sorts of things—tree trunks, coal, oil drums, cement, bricks, rods of pig iron. They are headed for factories or construction sites or the railroad station. The loads are so heavy that even though the carts are equipped with rubber tires, the porters have to strain to keep them moving.

Some are young men who laugh and joke as they haul their carts, and stop now and then for a friendly smoke

together. Others are old men and women, stooped and gray from a lifetime of hard labor. They plod along silently with bent heads, saving their breath for each step. Many are young women with seamed faces that already look old. Even girls and boys, scarcely eight years old, wearing tiny halters around their shoulders, trudge behind their mothers or fathers, their faces flushed with effort.

The porters make little money. In the bitter winters they shiver in their old threadbare clothes. On hot summer days each one carries a rag to wipe the sweat that streams down into his eyes. They are paid by the load, and they have to work from early dawn until dusk to earn enough to live on. Only when it is too dark to see do they return to their shacks on the outskirts of the city.

These armies of porters are hauling loads all over China, because the country is still so poor that it cannot afford to manufacture the millions of trucks needed to do the job. But the porters have a dream for their children. They dream of the day when China will be able to make all the trucks it needs. Then instead of being porters, their children will find work in factories, and their lives will be easier.

Beyond Tsinan the Yellow River flows through open country again. At last, more than a hundred miles away it descends through mud flats carrying along a final load of silt to the Gulf of Po Hai. It brings so much that each year the delta is extended a hundred yards or so farther out to sea.

The water is too shallow for a harbor here, and it is so muddy that it is difficult to tell ocean from land. It stretches away like a desolate plain to the distant horizon. And fishermen can be seen far out at sea casting their nets from stilts instead of boats.

CHAPTER 8

Harnessing the Yellow River

For almost three thousand miles we have followed the Yellow River on its course from the Kunlun Mountains of Chinghai to the Gulf of Po Hai. We have looked in on the people who live along its banks, and we have seen what they are doing to harness their unruly river.

There is much more yet to be done. It may take the Chinese as long as seventy years to finish it all. They are planning to build many more dams along the course of the river—at least fifty. When the work is done, five-hundred-ton junks will be able to travel from the mouth of the Yellow River to Lanchow, more than 1,500 miles by river to the west.

Behind the dams the reservoirs will store up floodwaters that will enable many more dry areas to be irrigated. But,

strangely enough, the Yellow River may not be able to provide the water for these reservoirs. Despite the havoc it causes, it actually contains less water than many smaller rivers. In years of prolonged drought, it has sometimes dwindled away to a mere stream.

The engineers have a daring remedy for this, which they will put into operation once all the dams are in place. They plan to split the upper course of the much fuller Yangtze and divert some of its water by canal to the Yellow River. The canal will bring four times as much water to the river as it now contains, but the series of dams will keep it from flooding.

Dams and reservoirs and extra water, however, will still not solve all the problems of the Yellow River. Already the thick layer of silt which the water is washing against the dams is beginning to clog the sluices. Over the years it will bring up the beds of the reservoirs until they, too, become useless.

The erosion must be stopped in the hills and the mountains and the plains. Trees anchor the soil in place and keep it from being washed away into the river. So all over China people are planting trees provided by the government forestry service and by farm communes. Tree nurseries cover many acres of land and contain billions of seedling trees. Many are fruit trees. Others are such fast-growing varieties as poplars.

The commune council sets a yearly quota of trees for

each member of the commune to plant. City people often spend their free time planting trees in the country. During their holidays, schoolchildren camp out on barren hills to plant a half-million trees at a time.

They plant them on the barren mountainsides and eroding hills of the Great Loess, on the North China Plain and the rain-scoured mountains of Shantung Province. So many trees have been planted across the dry northwest, as a barrier against the Gobi Desert sandstorms, that the tree belt is almost a thousand miles long and a mile wide.

And the work has only begun. The Yellow River people, young and old, are fighting a fierce battle to keep their countryside from running away to the sea. They are doing it all with trees.

HOW TO PRONOUNCE FOREIGN WORDS

Chinese is a difficult language for Westerners to pronounce. Many of the sounds in Chinese are not heard in western languages. This was the difficulty experienced by the first scholars who worked on phonetics.

There were other difficulties, too. There are many dialects in China. These dialects are so different from one another that people living in one part of the country cannot understand the language spoken by people living in a different locality.

However, all of China has the same written language. It is a form of picture writing called ideograph, or character. These characters have the same meaning throughout China, but they are spoken in different ways.

Today Communist China is trying to unify her people by teaching an official language. This official language has always been spoken in Peking, which is now the capital of Communist China, as well as in most of the north. The western world generally follows the official Chinese language in the pronounciation of words, names, and places in China.

Word	Pronunciation	Word	Pronunciation
Alashan	Ah-lah-shahn	Gautama Buddha	Gau-tuh-muh Bood-uh
Bayingol	Bi-yen-gaul	Gobi	Goh-bee
Chengchow	Jeng-joh	Han	Hahn
Chiang Kai-shek	Jee-ahng Ki-shek	Han Wu Ti	Han Woo Tee
Chientang	Jee-en-tahng	Hangchow	Hahng-joh
Chin Shih	Chin Shr	Hankow	Hahn-koh
Huang Ti	Huahng Tee	Hokow	Hoh-koh
Ching	Ching	Honan	Hoh-nahn
Chinghai	Ching-hi	Hopei	Hoh-bay
Chingtung	Ching-toong	Hsikan	Shee-kahn
Chu-fu	Choo-foo	Hsiung-nu	Shee-uhng-noo
Confucius	Kuhn-fyu-shus	Huang Ho	Huahng Haw
		Huangshui	Huahng-shway
Fen Ho	Fuhn Haw	Hui Hsin	Huay Shin

90

Word	Pronunciation	Word	Pronunciation
Kaifeng	Ki-fuhng	Ramadan	Ram-uh-dahn
kang	kahng		
Kansu	Kahn-soo	San Men	Sahn Muhn
kaoliang	kah-oh-lee-ahng	Shantung	Shahn-toong
Kublai Khan	Koob-li Kahn	Shansi	Shahn-shee
Kunlun	Koon-loon	Shensi	Shen-shee
		shuba	shuh-ba
Lanchow	Lahn-joh	Si-Kiang	Shee-Jee-ahng
Liu Ling	Lee-u Ling	Sian	Shee-ahn
Liuchia	Lee-u-jee-ah	Sining	Shee-ning
Lo	Law		
loess	loh-ess	Ta An	Dah Ahn
Loyang	Law-yahng	Tai Shan	Ti Shahn
Luliang	Loo-lee-ahng	Taihang	Ti-hahng
Lungmen	Loong-muhn	Takla Makan	Tah-klah Mah-kahn
Mao Tse-tung	Mao Dzuh-Doong	Tang	Tahng
		Tientsin	Tee-un-jin
Mengtsin	Muhng-tsihn	Touman	Toh-muhn
		tsamba	tsahm-ba
Nan Shan	Nahn Shahn	Tsinan	Jee-nahn
Nanking	Nahn-jing	Tsinling	Jin-ling
Ngolo	Ngaw-law		
Ningsia	Ning-shee-ah	Wei	Way
		Wu Tzu-tien	Woo Tsu-tee-un
Ordos	Ord-us		
		yak	yack
Paiyu	Pi-yoo	Yangtze	Yahn-tsee
Panaka	Pah-nah-kah	Yenan	Yen-ahn
Paotow	Bao-doh	Yi	Yee
Peking	Bay-jing		
Po Hai	Boh Hi		

Index

OCLC

Heterick Memorial Library
Ohio Northern University
Ada, Ohio 45810